AF490950

POLITICAL CONFUSION

Charleston, SC
www.PalmettoPublishing.com

Political Confusion

Copyright © 2023 by William Lawrence Drake

All rights reserved

No portion of this book may be reproduced, stored in a retrieval system, or transmitted in any form by any means—electronic, mechanical, photocopy, recording, or other—except for brief quotations in printed reviews, without prior permission of the author.

First Edition

Hardcover ISBN: 979-8-8229-0786-7
Paperback ISBN: 979-8-8229-0787-4
eBook ISBN: 979-8-8229-0788-1

— SAVING AMERICA III —

POLITICAL CONFUSION

WILLIAM LAWRENCE DRAKE

TABLE OF CONTENTS

POLITICAL CONFUSION

▲ ▲ ▲

SAVING AMERICA III

If history has taught anything, making the same mistakes occurs when knowledge is absent because of not paying attention to mistakes that were made in the past-And not paying attention to past mistakes has led to AMERICA BEING OUT OF CONTROL.

Race and politics are no different as each presents a mistake prone extrospection of viewpoints that are passed on by month from generation to generation – And from all appearance's the same kind of politics, and confusion are in play today.

When conflicts began between the North and South, Republicans represented the North, and Democrats represented the South – Today, predominantly African Americans occupy roles in the Democrat Party, and the remainder of America, and some independents, occupy the Republican Party – to prove that race plays a major role in politics, a recent example, (a true description) of a personal experience that occurred during a Primary Election in Dallas, Texas this year, will show how much Race is apart of the mind-set of some African Americans.

Voting by racial identity is racist, but it is also expected! When African Americans visit a polling place, race is used by other blacks to assume that they know how ALL blacks are going to vote - Without a word being spoken, in Dallas, Texas, during a Primary Election, as I approached the voting area, I was prejudged to be a Democrat because I am African American; the African American that made the assumption was puzzled after taking me to the wrong voting booth wherein the ballot that was entered into the machine was rejected.

After determining that I had mistakenly been taken to a Democrat voting booth, the person that was assisting me discovered that my ballot did not work because it was a Republican ballot - after re-examining my ballot the worker with a look of disdain, hate, and disappointment said, "YOU ARE A REPUBLICAN"! To add insult to injury, she said: "YOU SHOULD HAVE TOLD ME THAT YOU ARE A REPUBLICAN".

For a moment or two, I considered filing a complaint against the worker, but my better judgement told me to vote and move on – On other occasions, as I approached the voting area, black folks would approach me with voting materials for democrats that were seeking judgeships, and other positions, and to those folks, I simply said, no thanks for their efforts to give me voting instructions on how or who to vote for – The realization that because I am black, it was expected that I would be voting as a democrat is racist, but moreover it is expected by some blacks, and some whites, that my race determines my politics.

Some black folks vote for political parties because they have been told that is the way blacks vote – and for that reason alone, black poll workers assume that because one is black, that they are voting for the Democrat Ticket.

Conversely President Biden in an interview with a black man, said SOMETHING to the effect that "If you are considering voting for TRUMP, you ain't black"! Some black folks applauded the comments, and others laughed thinking that the remarks were funny. President Biden later offered a halfhearted apology, saying: "that he should not have been such a wise guy".

Democrats, around America, speak or think much like previous SLAVE OWNERS, when blacks were brought to Virginia as their property. The comments that President Biden makes are called GAFTS, his wife calls Latinos TACO'S, I WILL ASSUME THAT Dr. Biden makes GAFTS as well. The problem with the comments is not that they were spoken out loud, but that these ugly statements were though of at all!

I will not belabor the comments made by the President and THE FIRST LADY, but it is incumbent upon each of us to look at ourselves introspectively and decide what kind of country we desire to leave for OUR children, grandchildren, and great grandchildren. The "melting pot" is divided along racial lines, and from a personal perspective, racial issues run a close second to gender identity issues, that are being supported in public schools, and other public platforms.

Until observations about race and gender issues were brought to the forefront by politicians, these areas of concern by individuals were thought to be settled – It was believed and recognized that racial differences were behind most Americans; and many of us had agreed to let gays and lesbians decide how they wanted to live, without prejudgment.

Race and gender have emerged as political tools for folks that see a benefit in the political arena, or they desire to have power; and some seek to take advantage of others, especially African Americans, that don't agree with the politics of race or gender issues being taught in public schools.

RACIST AND HOMOPHOBIA

▲ ▲ ▲

Racist is defined as: "prejudiced against or antagonistic toward a person or people on the basis of their membership in a particular racial or ethnic group, typically one that is a minority or marginalized" - **Homophobia is defined as a "dislike or prejudice against gay people".** Without taking a political position on hate and prejudice, any clear-eyed person should agree that prejudice and hate are wrong, not partially wrong, but wrong legally, and politically.

Moral judgements have no legal place with respect to sex between consenting adults, the act is private and personal. In that lines have been crossed, and judgements made about race being taught in public schools, and gay and lesbian issues becoming political, now comes questions as to why race and gender are now political topics that appear in the public square – And specifically, why has race and gender issues become political?

So that the connection of the politics of race and gender is clearer, for persons that don't know why the connection is important, is to explain that race and gender topics are being taught in public schools to children that are too young to understand the topics - Public schools are no longer teaching reading, writing, math, science and history, and based on media sources, public schools are adopting social agenda platforms that add race and gender topics to the curriculum in lieu of teaching the basics.

Some folks will wonder why it matters to me, at 76, about what is being taught in public schools, my answer is that I pay taxes to support public schools, and my great-great grandchildren are attending public schools in Dallas, Texas - Should their educations call for explanations about sex and race, who is in the best position to teach them about those subjects that are more qualified than me.

Before I become illogical about the idea that strangers are, or may be instructing my great grandchildren about sex and racial bias, let me redirect my thoughts to scripture, and the Infallible Authority of GOD - It is realized that anger is not the best thing, but not being perfect sometimes makes it impossible to control my emotions.

I l Peter 1:20,21 says: (20) "Knowing this first, that no prophecy of the scripture is of any private interpretation… (21) For the prophecy came not in old time by the will of man: but holy men of God spake as they were moved by the Holy Ghost".

In times of personal crisis, and with respect to being negative in thought, having an alternative to anger is a Blessing, and a Curse. The blessing comes with the realization that the earth's survival depends on returning to God in prayer, understanding the importance of family, and loving America, a country that has been placed in our hands to care for and protect.

The curse evolves when PEOPLE place more value in/on THINGS, than they do in each other – For some, there is never enough of anything, and greed is the order of the day. For others, power and/or seeking power to determine to whom riches, property, food, health, and safety belongs is sought above respect for humanity.

Isaiah 55:10,11 reveals the truth about power, and it reads: (10) "For as the rain cometh down, and the snow from heaven, and reurneth not thither, but watereth the earth, and maketh it bring forth and bud, that it may give seed to the sower, and bread to the eater; (11) So shall my word be that goeth forth out of my month:

it shall not return unto me void, but it shall accomplish that which I please, and it shall prosper in the thing whereto I sent it".

The message clearly shows that real power is beyond the ability of man to control the important things in life – And it also proves that man is not as powerful as he thinks – the powers of humans is limited to being restrictive, and when restrictive powers are based on denying or preventing others from accomplishing success, it can be compared to the fact that a renter does not own the place he rents – In other words, nothing of value can be accomplished by saying THIS BELONGS TO ME, to include self and climate change.

The hope is that race, gender issues, and climate change can be settled without hostility towards one another, and people can be free to make individual choices as to how they live their lives; while at the same time understanding that public schools are not the place to teach about trans/homosexual sex, or racial bias, or oppression and climate change.

THE DRAG QUEEN SHOW IN PLANO TEXAS

▲ ▲ ▲

"KIDS ARE DELICIOUS: TEXAS DRAG QUEENS DANCE IN FRONT OF CHILD"

News sources report that parents sat through a drag queen show with their children to watch an exhibition of men and women dancing inappropriately in the presence of children. Sources also report that, not only did the parents clap and laugh at the performances, BUT THEY REMAINED SEATED UNTIL THE SHOW ENDED!

The drag queen shows in Plano, Texas was inappropriate for children to see, this observation is not a condemnation of the show for adults, and if the performance was not illegal for adult participants to enjoy, then so be it – however, as an attempt to create, or expand LBGTQ culture into the mainstream using children as the target audience, in my opinion, is wrong!

Somewhere in the civility of mankind is a need for adults to take measures to stop **culture wars;** and the politicization of sex and race gives us an opportunity to talk about how to stop culture wars now! I am no saint, but I know that the road to hell is paved with stupidity, ignorance, and arrogance – I am also aware that God is watching us, Hebrews 4:12 speaks to the power of God, and it reads "For the word of God is quick, and powerful, and sharper than any two-edged sword, piercing even to the dividing asunder of soul and spirit, and the joints and marrow, and is the discerner of the thoughts and intents of the heart".

FOR ADULTS ONLY: It is time to assess where each of our hearts are in matters involving belief in GOD, selection of friends, keeping families intact, and what America is to become futuristically. The seriousness as relates to matters of the heart will determine if our children can inherit peace, harmony, justice, and tranquility, in the America that WE leave to them to pass on to their children – And it does matter about relationships, love, trust, and charity; and forgiveness, directions, instructions, and traditions are needed to protect the futures of all human beings.

Former President Ronald Reagan said, "…it is important to believe in GOD, but it is also important that we believe in one another"; the evolution of America is being tested to see if, as a people, that we can enjoy together, the wonders, creations, and Blessings of GOD.

WHAT IS AT ISSUE WITH THE 1964 CIVIL RIGHTS ACT

▲ ▲ ▲

It is past time to have frank discussions about the differences between cultures, and life in America; and I am certain that total agreements about sex and race will not be graciously accepted by everyone in America, but it is important to open "pandoro's box" so that WE can face reality.

The Civil Rights Act of 1964, and the courts, gave LBGTQ CITIZENS Equal Rights legally, socially, and politically, but did not address, or create boundaries under the law, to outline, AND RESTRICT LBGTQ activities in relationship to children - gaining civil rights for the LBGTQ community should have come with rules, restrictions, and legal boundaries to protect children from obscene acts that appear to be recruitment actions of some LBGTQ people.

According to The Senate and Civil Rights: 1862-1963, the same passage of the 1964 Civil Rights Act was designed to help African Americans via civil means to have equal space in America; The US Senate Civil Rights Act of 1964 is said to have "…Marked a milestone in the struggle to extend civil, political, and legal rights and protections to African Americans, including former slaves and their descendants, and to end segregation in public and private facilities".

The Civil Rights Act of 1964, protects LBGTQ, and African Americans with coverage that prevents discrimination against both classifications of Americans – one classification deals with choice, and the other covers race – The irony is that choice, and birth are treated the same under the law. One classification includes a decision to make a private matter public, while the other, in most cases, is out of one's control.

1964 was a year in which SINGLE PEOPLE WITH CHILDREN came into existence – the impact on Marriage and morality gave rise to single moms that had children which were born out of wedlock, these single moms, on average, have three (3) children that are supported by the government - Presidents Lyndon Johnsons' introduction of THE GREAT SOCIETY legislation, is responsible for creating this problem.

Dr R. Claire Friend in his analysis of the 1964 Civil Rights legislation, opined that "It has been 50 years since Lyndon Johnson signed the Great Society program into law. Ten trillion dollars later, the effects have been the very antithesis of his stated aims. This single piece of public policy has destroyed the family, caused a marked increase in illegitimacy, crime, illiteracy, and drug abuse; and turned traditional America into a culture of fatherlessness".

According to Dr. Friend, in 2012, "the rate of illegitimacy was 5%. In that same period, children being born out of wedlock stood at 34 % for Anglos, 53% for Latinos, and 80% for African Americans".

According to USA Today, "unwed mothers make up a high number of welfare recipients, and many of the juveniles behind bars came from single moms". 1964, because of freedom to "DO YOUR THING", created the crisis that America faces in 2022 – Most major cities are faced with the results of policies that began with good intentions by a President 58 years ago, that DO NOT WORK IN 2022!

The Civil Rights Act of 1964, much like Roe vs Wade, may have outlived its time and usefulness – The 1964 Act was designed to prohibit discrimination on the basis of race, color, religion, sex, or national origin, but The Act has been used to discriminate by college admissions, create same sex marriages, while limiting the power of churches to participate in politics without being penalized – Let me again say that, in my opinion, the protections that gave rise to the Civil Rights Act of 1964 to protect Americans, are out of line/touch with what is needed today.

It appears that the 1964 Civil Rights Act stripped the rights of churches to participate in politics, while giving same sex partners, and college admissions administrators, the right to use sex and race to create an unlevel playing field – The government, to fix a problem, created a much larger problem in 1964.

THE IMPACT OF THE 1964 CIVIL RIGHTS ACT

▲ ▲ ▲

FOR ADULTS ONLY: Simply put America is facing a morality crisis that has far reaching legal ramifications; the government is complicit with respect to the legal aspects of this crisis by giving African Americans privileges, while discriminating against Anglos, and Asians, using race to grant African Americans opportunities, not on merit, but because of COLOR.

Same sex couples are permitted to marry, and adopt children, while religious organizations can be penalized for disagreeing with the lifestyles of same sex couples; if discrimination is wrong or illegal, why is the government permitted to use discriminatory practices under the guise of POLITICS to discriminate?

The government, using mandates, and judicial powers, has taken a position to create a crisis – using politics, and the powers of government to choose winners and losers; the 1964 Civil Rights Act made it policy to discriminate - why is this practice acceptable?

Instead of praising God for past Deliverances, growth, social evolution, and freedom, politicians have decided to become gods, but more than this, politicians are deciding to change history in 2022 – The facts are that Anglos are not willing to become slaves, be hanged, raped, and tormented by African Americans so that blacks can get even for having been enslaved!

America has been given a SECOND CHANCE to be a better nation, and not a nation of revenge, division, and confrontation. Psalm 107:1-9 sets an example of what needs to be a platform of peace going forward, and it reads: (1) O give thanks unto the Lord, for he is good: for his mercy endureths for ever. (2) Let the redeemed of the Lord say so, whom he hath redeemed from the hand of the enemy;)3) And gathered them out of the lands, from the east, and from the west, from the north, from the south. (4) They wandered in the wilderness in a solitary way; they found no city to dwell in. (5) Hungry and thirsty, their soul fainted in them. (6) Then they cried unto the Lord in their trouble, and he delivered them out of their distresses. (7) And he led them forth by the right way, that they might go to a city of habitation. (8) Oh that men would praise the Lord for his goodness, and for his wonderful works to the children of men! (8) For he satisfeth the longing soul, and filleth the hungry soul with goodness.

Time has come for America to grow up and stop being childish and stupid, Common Sense will not tolerate being silly as a way of life. And violence, and other crimes will not make America safer because politicians are willing to release criminals from prison, or simply not prosecute blacks that commit crimes.

Violence, as seen on video, and live television, looks inviting and courageous as black men push Anglos and Asians on to train tracks; these actions are being applauded by other blacks because it looks like black men are getting even for past discrimination - But it is dangerous when politicians, and other leaders in communities, look at crime as power, this is especially true when black criminals take advantage of SECOND CHANCES, and act as though they deserve an opportunity to take the lives, and property of others.

Politicians use black criminals as ponds, by taking the position that the criminal justice system has somehow been weaponized to "railroad" African American men to jails and prisons wrong-fully – Anglo politicians' empty jails, and support not prosecuting black criminals to get votes in Chicago, Maryland, New York, and California - and blacks that agree with these politicians, elect, and re-elect these politicians repeatedly.

The unforeseen tragedy when criminals are released from custody, or not prosecuted, is that these criminals return to "THE HOOD" where they are permitted to rob, rape, and murder other law-abiding citizens! Anglo politicians don't live in "THE HOOD", and for the most part, are not affected by the criminals they release.

Politicians also use black criminals to remain in power, and these politicians are considering legalizing Meth, Heroin, and Cocaine to enslave blacks, and others to preserve their hold on minority communities… GIVE THEM WHAT THEY WANT, if they stay in their neighborhood!

Politicians who believe in SECOND CHANCES for black criminals do so if these criminals remain in THE HOOD – The same concerns and understandings are held by people that live in MARTHAS' VINYARY, and the Hampton's; they support poor people, and want them to live anywhere but in their neighborhood.

GIVE THEM AN INCH, AND THEY WILL TAKE A MILE

▲ ▲ ▲

Approximately 58 years ago the 1964 Civil Rights Act introduced crime, fatherlessness, and sexual freedom to a people that were unprepared, and unknowledgeable about how a good intentioned law could be used to remove GOD, Morals, Values, and patriotism out of American homes and schools – From all appearances, the 1964 Civil Rights Act **looks like "GIVE THEM ENOUGH ROPE and see what happens"!**

Theoretically, the 1964 Civil Rights Act may not have been designed to corrupt American society but was instead designed to create an EVEN PLAYING FIELD for the disenfranchised; however, multiplication by lawyers and politicians erased all the good intentions with extraneous additions, such as, allowing boys to participate in girl's sporting events.

The 1964 Civil Rights Act when coupled with the Fourteenth Amendment was used to create ABORTION RIGHTS, abortion was changed to "WOMEN'S REPRODUCTIVE HEALTH", to avoid any negative politics associated with the word abortion.

It is noteworthy that the 1964 Civil Rights Act nor the Fourteenth Amendment to the United States Constitution, mentioned Abortion or boys participating in girl sports as a civil right.

Politicians and lawyers made abortion legal at the taxpayers' expense - The United States Supreme Court ruled in 2022 that decisions related to abortion should be returned to the states to manage – Politicians took up the mantle of abortion and made abortion a political football.

The question that comes to mind is: WHY SHOULD TAXPAYERS' PAY FOR THE SEXUAL DECISIONS OF AN ADULT WHEN THE DECISION MADE BY THE ADULT RESULTS IN PREGNANCY?

Sex and abortion is a choice that individuals make, why does the decisions of an individual to engage in such practices become the responsibility of politicians, and Americans that have abstained form the behavior that causes pregnancy?

THE RACIAL DIVISION CREATED BY THE 1964 CIVIL RIGHTS ACT

▲ ▲ ▲

Intended or not, the 1964 Great Society dream added racial insensitivity to America. It is not the purpose of this book to evaluate the intent of the Great Society, but it is the purpose, and responsibility of this work to measure the impact, and outcomes that The Great Society developed.

The history of 1960 reveals that America was still shaken, and responsive to segregation laws that emanated from President Eisenhower's reversal of segregated schools in 1957, at Central High school in Arkansas!

Central High school became the most dangerous campus in THE SOUTH when African American children took part in an attempt to integrate a Anglo high school – The issue of integration in Arkansas required Federal troop support and protection for African American children on September 4, 1957 as they attempted to enter Central High – Federal Troops were required because Governor Orval Faubus called in the Arkansas National Guard to block entry of Black students' entry into the high school.

Segregation was terminated on May 17, 1954, when the US Supreme court ruled that segregation in public schools was unconstitutional, "…The US Supreme Court said that separate is not equal …, and that segregation violated the Equal Protection Clause of the Fourteenth Amendment".

On one hand, this period in Americas' history, identifies, and frees a people that were field hands and sharecroppers in the South, who earned a daily salary of five dollars per day, for ten hours of work. While on the other hand, this history reflects how far America has come socially, and legally from 1954 to 2022.

The years notwithstanding, poverty, gang violence, robbery, rape, and murder has increased in many cities in America – Statically, poverty and racial issues have substantially become more fragile, and out of control, especially in African American, and Hispanic communities. If one listens to THE REASONS that crime has gotten out of control in minority communities, the loudest voices in the political arenas are suggesting that it is systemic racism.

Some citizens, to include scholars, blame the Criminal Justice System for creating a problem within the African American and Hispanic communities, because the police arrest black and brown youngsters for breaking the law - but at the risk of losing more friends, I will attempt to explain what I believe to be the ROOT CAUSE for crime, and racial divisions in America.

Rita Mae Brown is said to have coined the definition of insanity, she said "The definition of insanity referrers to preservation, which is the compulsive repetition of an action – not perseverance which is noble action" – The most used terminology, states that "the definition of insanity is doing the same thing over, and over expecting a different result" – I will not address the different definitions with a debate, but I will say that the 1964 Great Society political decision by former President Lyndon B, Johnson, had a hand in the origination of both, the social and criminal problems that are consuming America today!

FOR ADULTS ONLY: Crime and racial unrest that began with Anglos in the early development of America, has undergone revision and tolerance from 1954 to 2022: and the changes have exposed that positive transitions with respect to race and class in America are changed forever.

What has changed in 2022, is the fact that traditional relationships, (nuclear families), families with a father and mother, are no longer present in American society. As is evidenced by statistics, cities in the United States of America, have a proliferation of SINGLE PEOPLE WITH CHILDREN - The children that grow accustomed to living in family situations that consist of a promiscuous mother, and without a father, are now the new definition of a family.

Most often the children that find themselves in these non-traditional families, are heartless, antisocial psychopaths that rob, rape and murder other Americans with impunity. In Chicago, New York, Maryland, Philadelphia, and California, politicians have decided to divide the country into two parts, moral, and amoral – The ongoing problem that these political decisions have made are allowing rape, aggravated assault, murder, drug abuse, and domestic senselessness to exist in this country.

THE DESTRUCTION OF AMERICA IS AT HAND

▲ ▲ ▲

The idea that allowing crime to happen, will somehow fix the crime problem is ludicrous - And with all certainty, Christians must come from under a rock of acceptance that allows crime, Drag Queens, and Single People with Children to have legal protections, AND ACCEPTENCE! Christians should recognize that free reign with respect to allowing crime, Drag Queens, and Single People with Children to co-exist in America, is the beginning of destroying America.

To continue to overlook the impact of crime, Drag Queens and Single People with Children is allowing the next generation of Americans to think that crime is legal, that men can act like women, and that unmarried women are free to give birth to children at Taxpayer expense.

FOR ADULTS ONLY: Some politicians, and inner-city supporters of crime, Drag Queens, and Single People with Children think or believe that:

1. To speak out about crime is racist in that approximately 80% of criminals are black.

2. To not protect the choices of LGBTQ individuals is discrimination, and flies in the face of the 1964 Civil Rights Act, and Fourteenth Amendment.
3. Sexual freedoms are protected under the 1964 Civil Rights Act, and Fourteenth Amendment, and thereby allows women to have children at Taxpayer expense.
4. Abortions are protected under the Constitution, and taxpayers must pay for abortions.

If we look analytically at the above-mentioned thoughts and beliefs, each looks very much like politicians are deciding how to use vote harvesting within a targeted group to gain political advantages; to opine further, is to say that inner-city supporters, and participants in the above-mentioned ways to destroy America represent a dipropionate number of black and brown citizens.

Early on in this manuscript it was stated that the divisions in America would come about because of THE HAVES, AND HAVE NOTS, and that other divisions would be caused by political issues connected to governmental policies and mandates.

It is also at this time that I would ask the reader to recall that it was mentioned that politicians, inner-city supporters, and participants that seek to destroy America, are also against Christians and religious efforts to ask that the behaviors of criminals, and social dysfunctions of LBGTQ, SINGLE PEOPLE WITH CHILDREN, AND ABORTIONIST be stopped.

Politicians and participants in the destruction of America's effort have attempted to remove any religious influence that confronts the areas of destruction which America faces – The following methods have been employed to stop religious efforts to confront those that would destroy America:

1. Remove GOD and religious beliefs from all public platforms.
2. Weaken America militarily, and Defund the Police Efforts.

3. Allow criminals to walk away from crime without punishment.
4. Make the government the head of household in families.
5. Remove tax-free status of churches for political reasons.
6. Remove and displace morals and values with individualism.
7. Stop parents from taking part in the education process.
8. Allow negative outside influences to have power politically.

Failure to be vocal about the destruction of America has severe repercussions, in real terms, it means that apathy has become a major part of citizens' attitude about the future of America, God, Freedom, and Family.

The New York Times best selling author, Rick Warren, says "IT ALL STARTS WITH GOD". Rick Warren also says "…The purpose of your life is far greater than your own personal fulfillment, your peace of mind, or even your happiness. It is greater than your family, your career, or even your wildest dreams. If you want to know why you were placed on this planet, you must begin with GOD. You were born by his purpose, and for his purpose…"!

At the risk of losing more friends, I am not remaining silent while America forgets the Bible, the Constitution, The Declaration of Independence, The Family, and what can happen to the Future of America should good people, say nothing about the woke politics that are occurring in this country!

PRAISES FOR GOD'S ULTIMATE JUSTICE

▲ ▲ ▲

As can be clearly observed, within the last few pages of this manuscript, passages of scripture have been omitted, the omissions have been purposeful because the Bible, and scriptures will not be utilized to convert non-believers, or to make cheap political points.

Justice is found in truth, and truth alerts me that America is being destroyed from the inside out, and from top to bottom - America is at risk from the inside out because the word of God has been prosecuted and convicted by politicians, and America is being destroyed from top to bottom because morals, values, and integrity have been sublimated to crime, gender issues, and selfishness.

Psalm 9: 1-6 explains God's Ultimate Justice, and it reads: (1) I will praise thee, O Lord with my whole heart; I will shew forth all thy marvellous works. (2) I will be glad and rejoice in thee; I will sing praise to thy name, O thy most High. (3) When thine enemies are turned back, they shall fall and perish at thy presence. (4) For thou hast maintained my rights and my causes; thou satest in the throne judging right. (5) Thou hast rebuked the heathen, thou hast destroyed the wicked, thou hast put out their name for ever and ever.

(6) O thou enemy, destructions are come to a perpetual end, and thou hast destroyed cities; their memorial is perished with them".

FOR ADULTS ONLY: It is time to look at who benefits from racial oppression, as well as the people that are convinced by others that they are victims of racial oppression. As I think about victimhood in 2022, I am forced to examine race, political policies, common sense, and purpose, real or imagined, about blacks and racial oppression.

When race is investigated closely, it is important to decide what is more important – holding on too old friends or trusting factual truths. I have decided that factual truths are more important than keeping friendships alive – America's future is more important than friendships!

The most important viewpoint ever, is to look critically at history – the history of America will show that this country has evolved socially, and legally; this is not said to represent that everyone has been treated fairly in America, and I will not apologize for America's past, but I am willing to forgive EARLY AMERICA.

In terms of an assumption, some people benefit from "Let's Keep Hate Alive", this ideology has found prominence in 2022 America, and this ideology/attitude, if allowed to remain in OUR public space will destroy America!

Being black in America today is quite different from being black in America in 1952, the politics of race in America has been handed over to blacks to manage, maintain, and profit from – Some profiteers, that happen to be black politicians, radio, and television talk show host use their positions to cause young blacks to commit violent crimes, riot, and hate everyone, to include themselves! These same professional haters also support white politicians that keep hate alive, and both are destroying America.

Blacks that are guilty of directing this kind of young black insurrection do it for money; whites that support crime, riots, and insurrection by young black offenders, do it for power. Young black offenders have been led to believe that it is okay to rape, rob, assault others, and murder INTRARACIALLY!

To avoid name calling, and blaming others, I will simply say, "ENOUGH SAID" …But I will also warn that the kinds of street crime that are occurring presently will stop, or be stopped - Again, enough is enough!

All who persist in, or encourage, or create environments that are conducive to supporting crime in America will ultimately face GOD'S Ultimate Justice, however, the mode of transportation by which criminals and their supporters arrive before GOD will be determined on EARTH.

WHAT CAN BE DONE TO FIX AMERICA

▲ ▲ ▲

No Book can be complete without making recommendations as to how to fix those problems that have been raised in this manuscript– and my charge in being responsible to honor that expectation is no different than the expectation one gets after a doctors visit for medical treatment…HOW LONG DO I HAVE TO LIVE, WHAT WILL HAPPEN AFTER THE OPERATION, and HOW MUCH DOES THIS PROCEDURE COST?

For Adults ONLY: the answers about what can be done to "Fix America", are simple, and the fix begins with a return to GOD, understanding that THE FIX will not come from politicians, or other power brokers that believe the FIX should make them richer, or more powerful – The fix that is needed are outlined as follows:

- Help each other

- Always tell the truth

- Share

- Do your best

- Pay with hugs and kisses

- Listen to your parents

- Laugh at yourself

- Say I love you

- Try new things

- Be thankful

- Show compassion

- Be happy

- Love each other

- Dream big

- Respect one another

- Laugh out loud

- Keep your promises

- Say please and thank you

- Be grateful

- Think of others before yourself

- Use kind words

- Know you are loved

- Hug often

These fix America terms, and concepts came from an unknown author, more than likely from the internet, my wife left these remarkable objectives in our garage, I happen to see these objectives while sitting in the garage, wondering how to bring this manuscript to a close ...I WISH I COULD TAKE CREDIT FOR THIS MARVIOUS WORK, but I would then be no better than other plagiarist.

THANK YOU, AND GOD BLESS YOU

THE PERSONAL OPINIONS OF THE AUTHOR

▲ ▲ ▲

The author of this manuscript has struggle mightily with keeping political opinions, not found, or proven in or with the legal process out of this manuscript. And it has been extremely difficult not to opine or guess about the politization of DISTRACTIONS by the Biden Administration – However, it is fitting and proper to address my suspicions outside of the manuscript.

Recently, the President of the United States of America broke a long-standing tradition, policy, or position of America not to engage in PRISONER SWAPS – The President, his advisors, or his family broke with the practices of this LONG-STANDING position of not engaging in prisoner swaps with the exchange of Britney Griner for "THE MERCHANT OF DEATH's" release.

The Obama Administration made a swap for Bowe Bergdahl in a similar fashion during the Obama Administration's reign; both Presidents are Democrats, and from all appearances each President engaged in political decisions that involved enemies of the United States – The Obama Administration was involved with Iran, and President Biden is involved with Russia.

The political gauge, in terms of why these swaps happened is left to the reader, but logic points this writer to suspicions of a different kind; and both logic and suspicion tells me that both Presidents were protecting or shielding something or someone from prosecution and/or exposure. THE QUESTION IS WHY OR WHAT?

The WHEN question is documented by dates, but the WHY OR WHAT questions remain unanswered – All that is known is that one President wanted to apologize for America, and another President wanted to hide his family's involvement in influence peddling.

As an outsider, and a person that is not smart, it would appear that Congress would be interested in determining "Why and What" the purpose was for prisoner swaps for each president - This investigation would ensure that each president was looking out for the best interest of THE UNITED STATES of AMERICA, and not their own interest!

AMERICA CAN AVOID A
SECOND CIVIL WAR

▲ ▲ ▲

At present, it seems as though America is destined to fight a "SECOND CIVIL WAR", and it is not clear about how many fronts the war would include, for example, would the war be about Race, Gender, Class, The Have or Have nots, politics, religion, or abortion?

A lack of COMMON SENSE and logic, along with a composition of negative discussions related to climate change and gun control could in fact lead to a second civil war – But what would be accomplished by a war without an END? And what would winning look like?

My last appeal to America, and the world, is to not destroy the world as we know it! AND FOR HEAVENS SAKE, don't allow stupidity to rule or supplant MORALS AND VALUES that have saved this country from destruction.

FOR ADULTS ONLY: PLEASE READ CAREFULLY!

There is a reason that America has become frightened of its citizens, criminals control the streets, teachers can't teach, and discipline and integrity are lackluster terms that have no meaning – THE REASON FOR THE PROBLEMS THAT AMERICA

FACES TODAY ARE DETERMINED BY OUR LACK OF FAITH IN JESUS, GOD, AND THE BIBLE!

No faith transitions to no hope. No hope leads to chaos. Chaos allows stupidity to replace common sense. When common sense is replaced by no hope, and chaos, PEOPLE BECOME THEIR VERY OWN god's. EVERYONE ON THE PLANET IS IN CONTROL!

AND THE TOWER OF BABEL GROWS

www.ingramcontent.com/pod-product-compliance
Lightning Source LLC
Chambersburg PA
CBHW060924130726
48001CB00006B/2412